SCHOLASTIC

Instant Poetry Frames
Neighborhood & Community

by Betsy Franco

NEW YORK · TORONTO · LONDON · AUCKLAND · SYDNEY
MEXICO CITY · NEW DELHI · HONG KONG · BUENOS AIRES

Teaching *Resources*

For Lillian

Cover design by Jason Robinson
Interior design by Sydney Wright
Interior illustrations by Maxie Chambliss, James Graham Hale, and Sydney Wright

ISBN-13: 978-0-439-57629-1
ISBN-10: 0-439-57629-6

Copyright © 2008 by Betsy Franco
Published by Scholastic Inc.
All rights reserved.
Printed in the U.S.A.

1 2 3 4 5 6 7 8 9 10   40   15 14 13 12 11 10 09 08

Contents

Introduction

In *Instant Poetry Frames: Neighborhood & Community,* primary poets are encouraged to flex their creativity muscles and stretch their poetry skills. All this is done in the context of fun-filled, engaging poetry frames and starters that ensure success for everyone.

The poetry frames in this book focus on the neighborhood and community, so they fit right into your curriculum with no effort on your part. They are perfect for introducing, teaching, and reinforcing concepts your students are already studying.

The interesting and unique formats of the frames help children explore the concept of neighborhood from fall to summer, city to farm, day to night, and tiniest bug on the sidewalk to biggest homes on the block. The poetry frames about the community help children recognize the many different communities in their world: family, class, school, and the wider community.

Additionally, the poetry frames vary in complexity and in the amount of student participation, allowing you to individualize instruction. Children are asked to add only a word or short phrase in some frames, while they write the entire poem in others.

What Are Poetry Frames?

Poetry frames are quick and easy reproducible "invitations" into the world of poetry. They are simple, unfinished poems that invite students to complete them. Some have missing words or phrases, others consist of blank lines with helpful questions and tips. All of the frames included in this collection give children the comfort of writing within a structure. They also provide visual clues to help young poets brainstorm ideas and illustrate their own poetry.

Why Use Poetry Frames?

To build writing skills and meet the language arts standards.

Confidence makes all the difference when a child is writing poetry. The structure of poetry frames gives students the support they need while developing a wide range of writing skills. Frames motivate young poets not only to write, but also to keep writing! Using them helps children to:

* write in a variety of poetry forms
* organize their ideas
* sequence events
* use pictures to describe text
* focus on specific parts of speech
* apply mechanical conventions to their writing

* write for a variety of purposes (to entertain, inform, explain, and describe)
* edit and "publish" their work
* use prewriting strategies to plan written work
* and much more!

To present a variety of poetic forms.

In this collection, you'll find formal and informal poetic forms including riddles, limericks, haiku, and acrostic poems. There are also engaging frames for writing list poems, rhyming couplets, visual (or concrete) poems, and poems that give directions.

To individualize instruction.

The different frames require varying degrees of participation from students. Some ask children to fill in words, and others invite them to write an entire poem. This variation allows you to individualize instruction because it enables everyone to participate at his or her own level.

To encourage self-expression.

Using poetry frames enables students to share their preferences, opinions, feelings, and imaginations about their neighborhoods and communities. Children are, for example, encouraged to write about where they live, describe what they see out their window, explore the places and activities in their community, and tell how to build their perfect community. In addition, students are invited to use their imagination and creativity to write about things such as a silly, backward neighborhood or what happens when book characters come to life in the library. The frames also guide children in writing about the people around them—their family, neighbors, friends, and community workers. As they develop and personalize the poems, students can explore their lives and cultures, share details about their experiences, and express their imaginations.

To introduce basic elements of poetry.

Elements or poetic language are purposely interwoven throughout this book. Examples of personification, metaphor, simile, onomatopoeia, alliteration, and neologisms (made-up words) are included. Students are invited to use fun action words and interesting describing words to paint pictures with their language. They are also encouraged to play with different parts of speech—naming words (nouns), describing words (adjectives), and action words (verbs).

To build awareness of rhyme, rhythm, and repetition.

Poetry frames are simply poems that need to be finished. They are structured so that they will be fun to write and read aloud when completed. They often have a pattern of repeated phrase, or rhyming couplets or quatrains to begin and end poems. Some poems rhyme throughout, but in most cases, children don't have to worry about the rhyming—they can just enjoy reading their poems after completing them.

To integrate language arts, math, and science into your social studies curriculum.

All the poetry frames connect language arts to your social studies topics. In addition, some poems reinforce math skills, such as counting and 3-D shapes, while focusing on concepts related to neighborhood and community. Other poems encourage students to incorporate science concepts as they write about seasons, animals, and building a perfect community.

Using the Frames in Your Classroom

Each poem can be written individually, with partners, or as a class collaboration. Here's how you might use the frames with children:

1. Copy the frame of your choice for each student. Introduce the frame with the group before children begin. Review the directions together and write an example as a class.

2. Provide students with a copy of the reproducible frame and have them use pencils and crayons or markers to fill it in.

3. Circulate around the room to check that each child is engaged, helping to brainstorm when needed.

After poems are completed, celebrate kids' efforts by inviting them to:

* share their poem with a partner or a small group

* read their poem to the class or to an older buddy

* copy their poem onto a blank sheet of paper and illustrate it as part of a display

* make their poems into a class collaborative book for the classroom library

* display their poems on bulletin boards

* take home and share their poems with families

* write their poems on blank strips, display them in a pocket chart, and chant them with the class

* act out their poems

* create their very own anthologies by binding all their poems together

* hold a poetry reading in which each child reads his or her poem to the whole class

Connections to the Language Arts Standards

The activities in this book are designed to support you in meeting the following standards outlined by Mid-continent Research for Education and Learning (McREL), an organization that collects and synthesizes national and state standards.

Uses the general skills and strategies of the writing process:

• Uses writing and other methods (e.g., using letters or phonetically spelled words, telling, dictating, making lists) to describe familiar persons, places, objects, or experiences
• Writes in a variety of forms or genres
• Writes for different purposes (to entertain, inform, learn, communicate ideas)

Uses the stylistic and rhetorical aspects of writing:

• Uses descriptive words to convey, clarify, and enhance ideas
• Uses a variety of sentence structures in writing

Uses grammatical and mechanical conventions in written compositions:

• Uses conventions of print in writing (upper- and lowercase letters, spaces between words, writes from left-to-right and top-to-bottom)
• Uses complete sentences
• Uses nouns, verbs, adjectives, and adverbs in writing

• Uses conventions of spelling in writing (spells high frequency, commonly misspelled words from appropriate grade-level list; spells phonetically regular words; uses letter-sound relationships; spells basic short vowel, long vowel, r-controlled, and consonant blend patterns)
• Uses conventions of capitalization and punctuation in writing

Uses the general skills and strategies of the reading process:

• Uses mental images based on pictures and print to aid in comprehension of text
• Uses basic elements of phonetic analysis (common letter/sound relationships, beginning and ending consonants, vowel sounds, blends, word patterns) to decode unknown words
• Uses basic elements of structural analysis (syllables, compound words, spelling patterns) to decode unknown words
• Understands level-appropriate sight words and vocabulary
• Uses self-correction strategies (searches for cues, identifies miscues, rereads, asks for help)
• Reads aloud familiar stories, poems, and passages with fluency and expression
• Understands the ways in which language is used in literary texts (personification, alliteration, onomatopoeia, simile, metaphor, imagery, rhythm)

Source: Kendall, J. S., & Marzano, R. J. (2004). *Content knowledge: A compendium of standards and benchmarks for K–12 education.* Aurora, CO: Mid-continent Research for Education and Learning. Online database: http://www.mcrel.org/standards-benchmarks

Instant Poetry Frames

Neighborhood & Community

A neighborhood has many kinds of homes.
Finish this poem about homes.
Use opposites or words that are different from each other.

Homes in a Neighborhood

Homes can be _____.
Homes can be small.
Homes can be _____.
Homes can be wide.

Black or _____.
Wooden or _____.
Old or _____.
Cozy inside.

On water, on _____.
Near _____, near _____.
With _____, with _____.
With a sidewalk outside.

With a pet or with no pet,
With trees, with no trees,
Your home is your home.
Sun up to sunset!

by _____

What do you like about your neighborhood?

Describe what you like about it. Surprise the reader by what you say.

Example: *When it's fall, the brown shriveled leaves talk to me.*

When the crows caw, my neighborhood is a lush rainforest.

To help you be surprising include:
* one of the seasons of the year
* the name of a neighbor
* a form of transportation
* a color
* a sound
* a bug or animal

What I Like About My Neighborhood

When _____

_____.

When _____

_____.

When _____

_____.

When _____

_____.

When _____

_____.

by _____

A list poem is made up of an interesting list of descriptions or events.
Write a list poem about a silly, backward neighborhood.

Example: *In my silly, backward neighborhood,*
the mice get together and chase the cats,
and the trees and flowers grow roots for hats.

Use the questions in the box to get you thinking.

* What do the bugs and animals do?
* What happens in different seasons?
* How do kids ride their bikes?
* How do the houses and yards look?

In My Silly, Backward Neighborhood

In my silly, backward neighborhood,
adults wear pajamas all day long,
and the teachers love when our answers are wrong.

_____

_____

_____

_____

_____

The roofs of the houses are on the ground.
And the balls bounce up but never down!

by _____

Most neighborhoods change in every season.

Choose a season. Write about your neighborhood in that season.

Write the name of the season in the title and on the short lines of the poem.

Example: *I am the neighborhood in fall.*

I am the leaves flipping and twirling like acrobats.

You can use the questions in the box to get you thinking.

＊ What do you see in this season?   ＊ What do kids play?

＊ What colors do you see?   ＊ What do adults do?

＊ What things do you smell?   ＊ What does nature do?

The Neighborhood in _____

I am the neighborhood in _____.

I am the _____.

I am the _____.

I am the _____.

I am the _____.

I am the _____.

I am the neighborhood every _____.

by _____

The poem in the box is called a *limerick*.
The three underlined words rhyme.
The two short lines also rhyme.

Write a limerick about your neighborhood.

1. Write *girl* or *boy* in the first blank.
2. Write a street name in the second blank.
3. Follow the rhyme pattern of a limerick to fill in the lines.
4. Draw a picture to go with your limerick.

Neighborhood Limerick

A young _____ from _____ Street

_____ .

_____ ,

_____ .

_____ .

by _____

Poets look at and listen to things very carefully.
Look out the window at home or school.
What do you see? What do you hear?
Use details to write a poem about what you see and hear.

Example: *Out my window I can see*
white dandelion parachutes blowing in the wind.

Out My Window

Out my window, I can see

_____

_____

_____.

That's what you'd see if you were me.

Out my window, I can hear

_____

_____

_____.

That's what you'd hear if you used my ears.

That's what you'd hear,
and that's what you'd see,
if you looked out my window,
so carefully!

by _____

A poem can be a list of words arranged in an interesting way.
Write the names of things you might see as you walk around
your neighborhood.
Write the words on the streets in the picture.
Examples: *stones*
         cracks in the sidewalk
         roly-poly bugs

Walking Down the Street

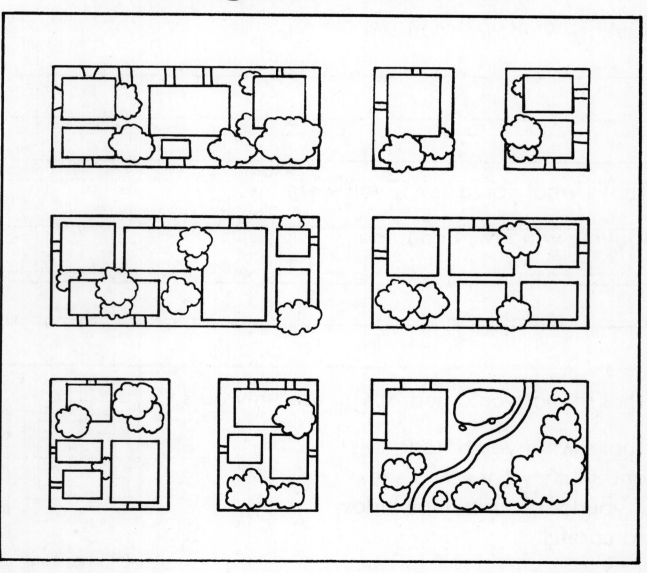

by _____

Instant Poetry Frames: Neighborhood & Community © 2008 by Betsy Franco, Scholastic Teaching Resources

In an *acrostic* poem, the first letter of each line is used to spell out a special word.

This is an acrostic poem that uses the word *fish*:

    Fins
    In water
    Scales
    Hiding at the bottom

Write an acrostic poem about your favorite animal in the neighborhood. Use each letter in its name to start a line in the poem.

Animal Acrostic

_____

_____

_____

_____

_____

_____

_____

by _____

Your neighborhood is different in the day and in the night.
Use words that paint a picture to finish the poem.
Example: *In the day, I hear lawnmowers rumbling across yards.*
In the night, I hear crickets chirping in the bushes.

Day and Night

My neighborhood changes
from day to night.
I hear different sounds,
and I see different sights.

In the day, I hear _____

_____.

In the night, I hear _____

_____.

In the day, I see _____

_____.

In the night, I see _____

_____.

My neighborhood changes
from day to night.
The neighborhood is different
in dark and in light.

by _____

Look outdoors around your neighborhood or school.
Find something special in nature and write a *haiku* about it.
Draw a picture to go with your haiku.

A haiku has three lines.
Try to use the number of syllables shown here for each line:

Tulip

Like a silken cup (5 syllables tell what it looks like)

waiting to catch fresh raindrops (7 syllables tell something about it)

in the spring drizzle (5 syllables tell what time of year you see it)

Neighborhood Nature Haiku

_____

_____

_____

by _____

In a *couplet*, every two lines rhyme.
Think about what people and animals do at a park.
Then use action words that rhyme to finish this couplet.
You can use words in the box to help you,
or use words of your own.

At the Park

Sunning
Running

Swinging

_____

_____

_____

_____

_____

Walking a dog,
Taking a jog,

at the park
'til it's dark.

by _____

Instant Poetry Frames: Neighborhood & Community © 2008 by Betsy Franco, Scholastic Teaching Resources

Write a poem that describes a country farm.
Write about what a visitor might see, smell, hear, feel, and taste.
Use unusual and made-up words.
Example:
Touch the duffy feathers of a sun-yellow chick.

Come Visit the Farm

Come visit the farm
with its weather-worn barn.

See the _____

_____.

Smell the _____

_____.

Hear the _____

_____.

Touch the _____

_____.

Taste the _____

_____.

A day on a farm is hard to forget.
And you just might take home
a soft, fluffy pet!

by _____

A city neighborhood has lots of sounds.
Write fun sounds in the blanks.
Make up words!
Draw pictures around your poem.

Sounds in the City

Sounds in the city.
Hear the songs
as the city life bustles along.

_____, _____,

The cars go by.

_____, _____,

Street musicians play.

_____, _____,

The jackhammer's tune.

_____, _____,

People talking all day.

_____, _____,

Trains pick up speed.

City sounds!
Yes, indeed!

by _____

Write a *counting* poem about a neighborhood.
Make your lines longer than 2 words.
Draw some of the things you wrote about.
Example: *Four barking pups pulling at their leashes.*

Counting in the Neighborhood

Counting in the neighborhood, 1, 2, 3.
One mail carrier we wait to see.

Two _____.

Three _____.

Four _____.

Five _____.

Six _____.

Seven _____.

Eight _____.

Nine _____.

Ten _____.

We count in the neighborhood 1, 2, 3.
Hey, there's one of you and one of me!

by _____

Write about what the sidewalk would say if it could talk.
To get started, think about what the sidewalk might feel about:

    ✳ the people and animals that use it   ✳ where it goes
    ✳ things that travel along it   ✳ what grows around it

Example: *I like the way scooters tickle me as they zip along my tummy.*

The Sidewalk Speaks

Have you ever given a thought
to your friendly sidewalk?
I have all kinds of different feelings,
and I finally get to talk.

I _____

_____.

I _____

_____.

I _____

_____.

I _____

_____.

I'm glad to be here for everyone.
I'm absolutely free.
Think about it—
What would you feel
if you didn't have me?

by _____

Imagine your neighborhood has a newspaper.
Make up headlines to write on each line of the poem.

Example: *Snoop the Dog Eats Mrs. Pear's Birthday Cake*
Kids Play Kickball Under the Moon
Bakery Has New Tangy Strawberry Tart

The Neighborhood News

Now for a report on the neighborhood news.
It's action-packed, and it won't make you snooze.

_____

_____

_____

_____

_____

_____

_____

We're bringing the fast-breaking news to you.
That's all today for the neighborhood news!

by _____

It's fun to pretend that nonliving things are alive.

Write an ending for each line of the poem.

Example: *When the trucks galloped down the road,*
the sidewalk hopped to keep up with them.

Use words from the box. Or use words of your own.

✳ crawled	✳ laughed
✳ rolled	✳ played
✳ skipped	✳ twirled
✳ tiptoed	✳ flipped

The Mixed-Up Neighborhood

One day in the mixed-up neighborhood,
nothing was acting the way it should.

When the sidewalk _____,

the yard _____.

When the STOP sign _____,

the street _____.

When the house _____,

the roof _____.

When the street light _____,

the fence _____.

When the car _____,

the garage _____.

Thank goodness, everything was acting as it should,
When night came to the neighborhood!

by _____

Write a five-line poem called a *diamante.*

1. Read the poem in the box.

2. Look at the kind of words used in each line.

3. Write a diamante about your neighborhood. Your poem will look like a diamond if you write only on the lines.

My neighborhood
wide-open, earthy
plowing, planting, harvesting
proud, joyful, tired, caring
Farms

My Neighborhood

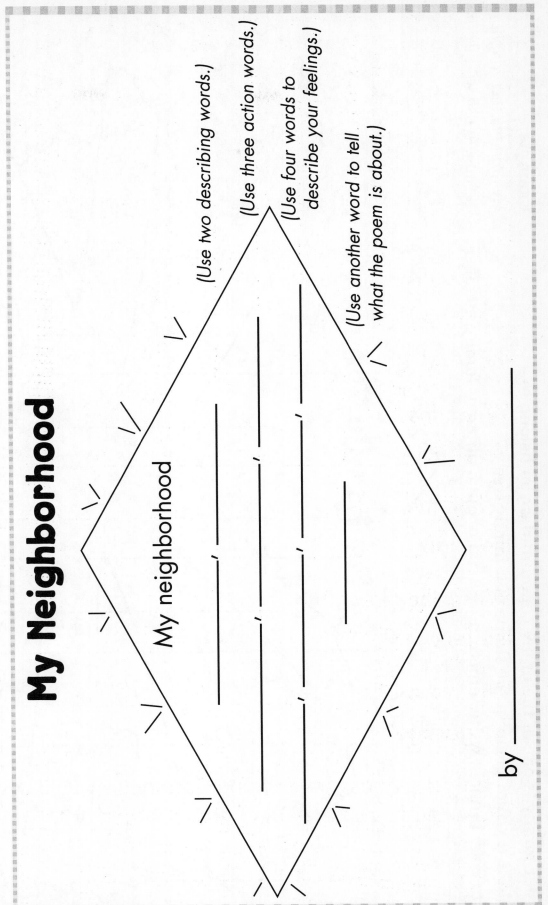

My neighborhood

(Use two describing words.)

(Use three action words.)

(Use four words to describe your feelings.)

(Use another word to tell what the poem is about.)

by _____

Instant Poetry Frames: Neighborhood & Community © 2008 by Betsy Franco, Scholastic Teaching Resources, page 25

Your family is one of the many communities you belong to.

Make a visual poem in the shape of a family tree.

On each branch, write something special about a different family member.

Example:

My grandmother taught

me how to fish with worms.

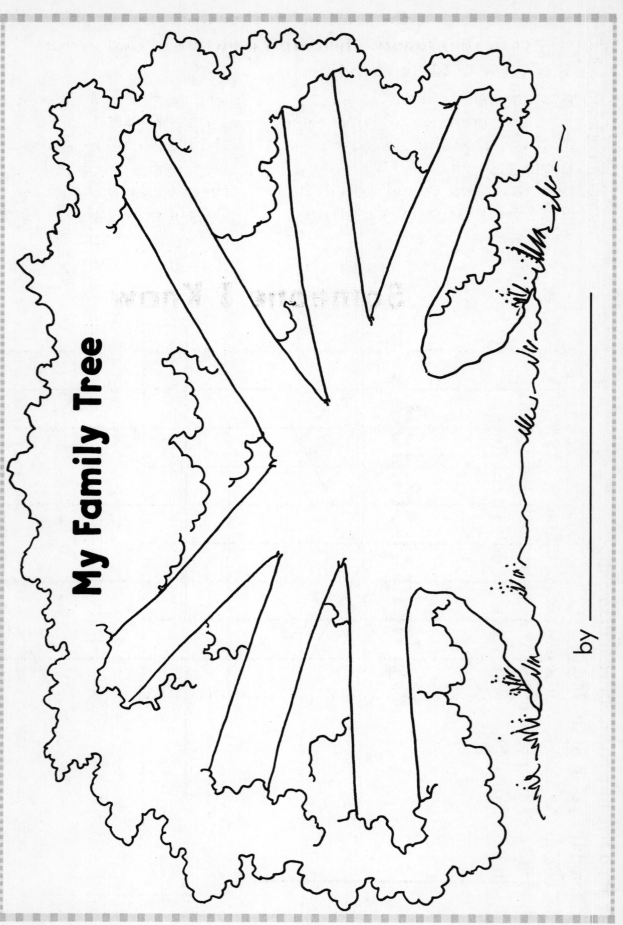

My Family Tree

by _____

Instant Poetry Frames: Neighborhood & Community © 2008 by Betsy Franco, Scholastic Teaching Resources, page 26

**Write a poem to describe someone in your community
who is not in your family. Then draw a picture of that person.
Use this guide to fill in each line:**

Compare the person to an animal.
Compare the person to a seasonal thing.
Tell what you like about the person.
Describe the person.
Tell what makes the person special.
Tell about something you've observed
    the person say or do.

Mrs. Singer is a gentle lamb.
She is a daffodil in spring.
She always gives us lemonade.
She has long gray hair and squinty eyes.
She has a dog that limps.
On Halloween, she lets us pick our treats.

Someone I Know

_____ is _____.

_____ is _____.

_____

_____.

_____

_____.

_____

_____.

_____

_____.

by _____

You spend time with your classroom and school communities.
Helping each other in these communities can make them
feel warm and friendly.
Fill in the first six lines with the names of different people in your class.
Then fill in the other blanks to finish the poem.

Our Classroom Community

I help _____.

_____ helps _____,

_____ helps _____,

_____ helps _____,

_____ helps _____,

and _____ helps me.

We help each other
with our reading,

with our _____,

and with our

_____.

With all that helping,
don't you see—
We make a class community!

by _____

Use your senses to describe the playground during recess.

* Questions *

 ❋ What noises do you hear?   ❋ What things do you touch?
 ❋ What things do you see?   ❋ What things do you smell?

The Playground Scene

There are sights and there are smells.
There are things to touch.
It's swell!

I see _____

_____.

I smell _____

_____.

I feel _____

_____.

But most of all, there are so many sounds,

such as _____

and _____.

The playground sounds are all around.

Things to see,
smell, and touch,
and sounds to hear—
all abound!

        by _____

What happens in the classroom after the last day of school?
Pretend that the school supplies have a good-bye party.
Use alliteration—write words that begin with the same sound.
Draw pictures to go with your poem.

Examples: *The pencils prance around the playground.*
The rulers run and race.

Good-bye Party

When school is over for the year,
the school supplies wake up and cheer.

The _____.

The _____.

The _____.

The _____.

The _____.

The _____.

When you return the very first day,
the supplies go back to their school-time ways.

by _____

Instant Poetry Frames: Neighborhood & Community © 2008 by Betsy Franco, Scholastic Teaching Resources

In a poem, it's always good to include details.
Which is more interesting?

My family goes places.

My family goes to the bowling alley.

In the poem, include interesting details about the place you live.

The Place Where I Live

I live in _____, _____.
           (city)   (state)

How about you?

Going to _____ is a really fun thing to do.

My friends and I like _____.

It's a wonderful place to play.

Community helpers like _____

watch out for us every day.

Whenever I _____,

I know it will be great.

_____, _____
    (city)   (state)

is a place that's just first-rate!

by _____

The community is like a patchwork quilt.
Write about people in your neighborhood,
at school, or in the bigger community.
Tell something interesting about each person.

Example:
*There's Mrs. Stone,
who shoots hoops with
us on her driveway.*

My Community Is a Quilt

My community is a quilt
with folks all over it.
Each person is very different
but everybody fits.

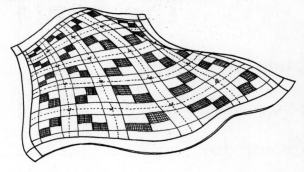

There's _____, who _____

_____.

There's _____, who _____

_____.

There's _____, who _____

_____.

And there's _____, who _____

_____.

All these people fit together
to make a special quilt.
When we all add something different,
our community is built!

by _____

Instant Poetry Frames: Neighborhood & Community © 2008 by Betsy Franco, Scholastic Teaching Resources

Write a short story about a favorite place in the community.
Underline 15 to 20 key words in the story.
Then use the words to write a poem.
Use 2 or 3 of the words on each line. Add other words if you need to.

My Favorite Place

My favorite place in the community is _____.

When I go there, I _____

_____

_____

_____

_____

_____

My Favorite Place Poem

_____

_____

_____

_____

_____

_____

by _____

Write a poem about the 3-D shapes found around your community—
spheres, cones, cylinders, rectangular prisms, pyramids, and cubes.

Example: *See the big red rubber balls bouncing on the playground.*

Think about the different shapes you might see:

* in stores * in houses * at school * outdoors

Shapes in the Community

Circles and spheres,
around and around,
in the sky and on the ground.

See the _____.

See the _____.

Cylinders and cones, big and small.
Cones and cylinders, short and tall.

See the _____.

See the _____.

Rectangular prisms, pyramids, cubes—
look inside and out, at different views.

See the _____.

See the _____.

Shapes are just waiting to be found.
3-D shapes are all over town.

by _____

It's fun to make up words to use in a poem.

How can you make up a word? Here are some ideas:

- Change one or more letters in a word: *bounce* can become *jounce*.

- Take a letter like *Z* and make up a word such as *zamboozle*.

- Put two words together: *rumble* and *rush* can become *rumblerush*.

Now write a poem about different ways to get around in a community. Include made-up words!

You can use words in the box to help you get started.

* Action Words *

| * chug | * dart | * dash | * race | * soar | * speed |
| * streak | * swerve | * swish | * swoosh | * zip | * zoom |

Zipping Around Town

The bus jounces up and down over bumps in the road.

The skateboard _____.

The scooter _____.

The bicycle _____.

The car _____.

The truck _____.

The train _____.

The plane flooooooms down the runway and up to the sky.
So many wheels zipzoaring by!

by _____

Community helpers are at work during the day and at night.
Write a thank-you poem to let them know you care.

Thank You, Community Helpers

Thanks to our helpers for the things they do.

Here are some notes to thank just a few:

Thank you, police officer,

for _____.

Thank you, librarian,

for _____.

Thank you, teacher,

for _____.

Thank you, mail carrier,

for _____.

Thank you, doctor,

for _____.

Thank you, baker,

for _____.

Thank you, firefighter,

for _____.

To community helpers in our town,
I give you cheers all around.

by _____

Instant Poetry Frames: Neighborhood & Community © 2008 by Betsy Franco, Scholastic Teaching Resources

Write a *riddle* poem about a community helper.
Choose a community helper from the box,
or think of one of your own.
Give two or three clues about the community helper.
Example: *From my head to my toes*
I'm covered in flour.
I start baking cakes
at an early hour.
Who am I? (baker)
Now write your own riddle poem and give it to a friend to answer!

* police officer
* doctor
* postal worker
* teacher
* firefighter
* newspaper reporter

Community Helper Riddle

_____

_____

_____

_____

_____

Who am I? _____

by _____

It's so exciting to get something in the mail!
Imagine what the mail carrier might bring you.
Make up people or use real people in your poem.
Draw a picture to go with your poem.

Example:
*If I got a letter from
my cousin Joe,
it might tell me about
his skateboard tricks.*

What Will the Mail Carrier Deliver?

If I got a letter from _____,

it might _____.

If I got a postcard from _____,

it might _____.

If I got a package from _____,

it might _____.

If I got a birthday gift from _____,

it might _____.

Even if I get no mail today,
I'll write a friend anyway,
so my friend can have
an exciting day!

by _____

Instant Poetry Frames: Neighborhood & Community © 2008 by Betsy Franco, Scholastic Teaching Resources

What happens in the library at night?
Do the book characters come out to play together?
Fill in the blanks to tell what they do.

Use characters from the box, or use your own.

* Cinderella   * the three little pigs   * Curious George
* Clifford   * the gingerbread man   * Junie B. Jones
* Stuart Little * Encyclopedia Brown   * Arthur

In the Library at Night

You're bound to see a crazy sight
if you visit a library late at night.

Harry Potter and _____
dive and swoop aboard his broom.

_____ and _____
_____ in the room.

_____ and _____
_____ and have some fun.

_____ and _____
_____ 'til they see the sun.

Then everyone goes back to their books,
and the library looks like it always looks.

by _____

Instant Poetry Frames: Neighborhood & Community © 2008 by Betsy Franco, Scholastic Teaching Resources

Write a poem that advertises an ice cream store in the community.
Make up words that tickle your tongue to describe each flavor.

Examples: *soft-as-silk butterscotch*
tickle-your-tummy peppermint

Here are some describing words to help you get started:

✳ creamy	✳ soft	✳ thick	✳ sweet	✳ lumpy
✳ smooth	✳ tangy	✳ sour	✳ crunchy	✳ cool

Our Ice Cream Store

At our ice cream store,
what will you try?
Just take your pick—
so many flavors to buy:
tickle-your-tummy peppermint

_____

_____

_____

_____

So step right up.
Our cold ice cream
is everybody's
yummy dream!

by _____

Instant Poetry Frames: Neighborhood & Community © 2008 by Betsy Franco, Scholastic Teaching Resources

The pet store is a lively place.
On each line, describe an animal and tell what it is doing.
Write the name of the animal you would choose on the last line.
Then draw a picture of it.

Example: *The black puppy is sticking its paws through the cage.*
The hamster is circling around like a track star.

You can describe some of these pets, or use other pets:

✳ puppy   ✳ snake   ✳ parrot   ✳ kitten   ✳ turtle   ✳ hamster   ✳ goldfish

Lively Pet Store Scene

The store is full of so many pets.
Which one of the special pets will I get?

The furry kitten _____

_____.

The _____

_____.

The _____

_____.

The _____

_____.

It's a very hard choice to make,

but the _____

is the one I'll take!

by _____

Write a poem that describes the sights and sounds of a parade.
Use words that spell out the sounds you would hear.

Example: *Cymbals clash.*

You can use the words in the box, or use your own words.
Draw some of the noise-making things around
your poem.

* toot	* pop
* ping	* buzz
* tweet	* honk
* bang	* bonk
* boom	* whiz

The Parade

Parade! Parade!
Here it comes.
The very first thing I hear is drums.

_____

_____

_____

_____

_____

_____

Parade! Parade!
What a treat.
Join the fun.
March down the street!

by _____

A poem can be a conversation.
Write about a conversation with your community.
Tell about the interesting things it has to offer.
Ask a friend to help you read your poem out loud to the class.

Hey, Community

Hey, there,
community.
Let's talk—
just you and me.

Hey, what can I do around here when I'm bored?

You can _____.

Hey, what can I do around here when I feel adventurous?

You can _____.

Hey, what can I do around here when I feel full of energy?

You can _____.

Hey, what can I do around here when I'm with my friends?

You can _____.

Hey there,
community.
You're pretty cool—
We all agree!

by _____

Interview an older person.

Ask the person to tell about the community he or she lived in as a child.

Draw a picture of something described in your poem.

Questions to ask:

✳ How is your community different today? ✳ How did people travel?

✳ How did you get to school? ✳ What were the homes like?

✳ What did you do for fun? ✳ What were your favorite places to go?

Long Ago

I talked to _____
who had some things to say
about what the community was like
in those long ago childhood days.

_____

_____

_____

_____

_____

_____

Some things were very different
in communities long ago.
I wonder if we'd recognize
the communities we now know.

by _____

Write directions for building
a perfect community.
Choose whatever places you'd like!

Think about where people would:
* go to get help   * live
* go to have fun   * buy food
* get medical care * relax

Building My Perfect Community

I'll build a community.
That's what I'll do.
And here are directions
I'd give to my crew:

First, build _____

because _____.

Next, make _____

where kids can eat.

Next, we'd need _____

because _____.

Then, a _____

for fun would be neat.

And a _____

would please everyone.

Finally, don't forget _____

before you're done!

by _____

What things in your world would be hard to live without?

Write about specific things you would miss.

Draw a picture to go with your poem.

Example: *Imagine my home without my scruffy old stuffed giraffe.*

Imagine

Imagine my . . .

home without _____.

street without _____.

neighborhood without _____.

class without _____.

school without _____.

community without _____.

world without _____.

I'm happy and I'm grateful
for the way things are.
I'm happy and I'm grateful
for my world near and far.

by _____

Instant Poetry Frames: Neighborhood & Community © 2008 by Betsy Franco, Scholastic Teaching Resources

What do you think your community will be like in the future?
Use your imagination to fill in the lines.
Then draw a picture of yourself in your future community.

In the Future

For sure in the future,
things are bound to change.
I'll tell you how I think they'll be,
though you might find it strange.

To get to school, kids will ride _____ every day.

Instead of books, they'll _____.

They'll _____ when they play.

Food will be _____

and cars will run on _____.

A robot will _____
instead of you.

What do you think?
Will this come true?

by _____

Notes